LANDMARK NORTHAM

BONE HILL:
Northam's Best Kept Secret

by

JIM JACKSON

Typeset/Design by Jonathan Downes,
Proofed by Ross Collier
Graphics by Barry Payne
Cover and Layout by SPiderKaT for CFZ Communications
Using Microsoft Word 2000, Microsoft Publisher 2000, Adobe Photoshop CS.

First published in Great Britain by CFZ Press

CFZ Publishing Group
Myrtle Cottage
Woolsery
Bideford
North Devon
EX39 5QR

ISBN: 978-1-909488-00-7

To Counsellor Andrew Eastman, whose ebullient and contagious enthusiasm for local history inspired me to compile this brief volume.

ACKNOWLEDGEMENTS

Mr Ross Collier
Mr Jon Downes
Mrs Corinna Downes
Ms Janet Hazel
Mr Andrew Lambert
Mr Barry Payne
Mr Cyril Williams
Mrs Jane Whittaker

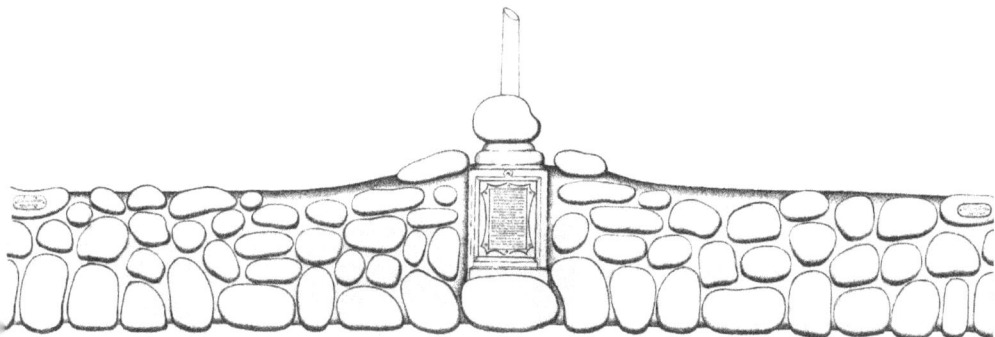

THIS FLAGSTAFF
AND CAIRN OF SIXTY BOULDERS
BOUGHT HITHER BY WILLING HANDS
FROM THE FORESHORE OF BIDEFORD BAY
ARE ERECTED BY THE INHABITANTS
OF NORTHAM AND WESTWARD HO!
TO COMMEMORATE THE COMPLETION
OF THE 60TH YEAR OF THE
REIGN OF HER MOST GRACIOUS MAJESTY
VICTORIA
QUEEN OF THIS REALM ⅂ EMPRESS OF INDIA
AND ARE INTENDED AS A JOYFUL MEMORIAL
OF THANKFULNESS TO ALMIGHTY GOD
FOR THE BENEFICENCE
OF HER RULE
THE 22ND DAY OF JUNE 1897

"MAY THESE STONES NEVER BE WITHOUT
BRAVE AND PIOUS MARINERS
WHO WILL COUNT THEIR LIVES AS WORTHLESS
IN THE CAUSE OF THEIR COUNTRY
THEIR BIBLE AND THEIR QUEEN – AMEN"

KINGSLEY'S WESTWARD HO!

NOW

1837

Queen Victoria
died
Jan 22nd
1901

The Battle Day is

Now

Past

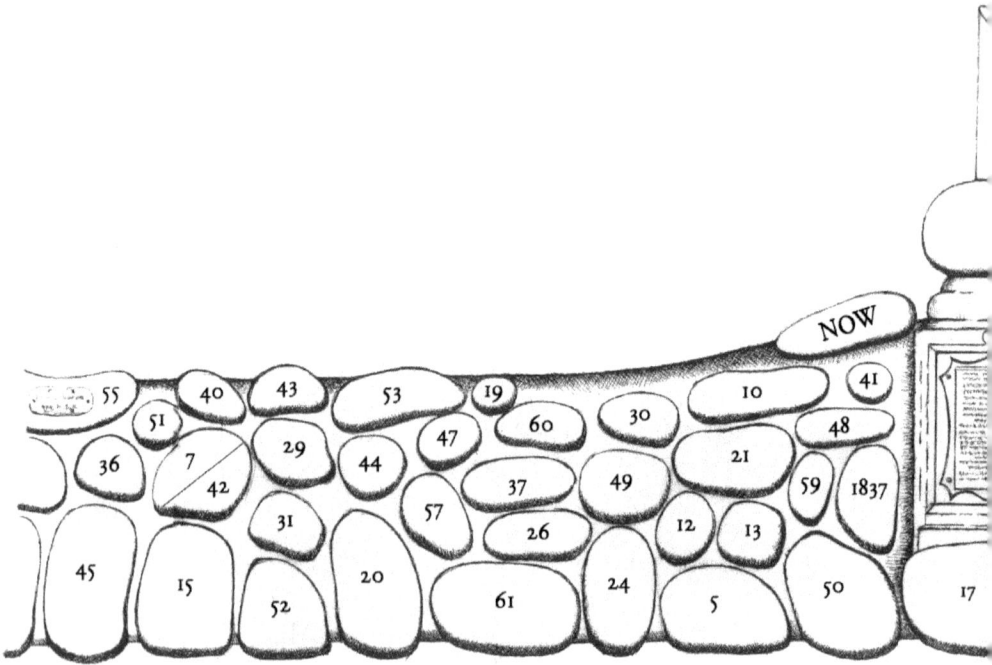

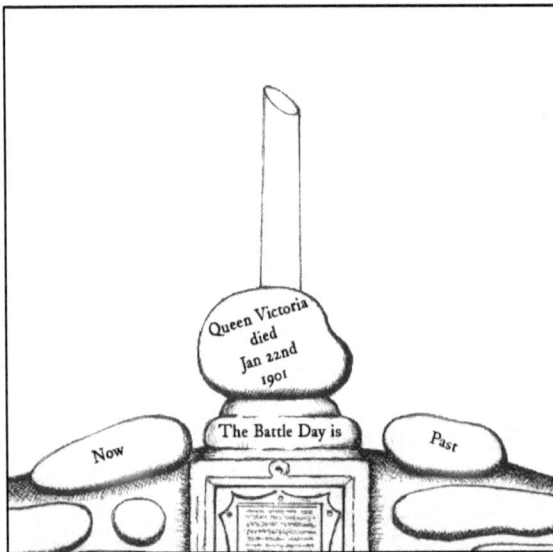

1. ANSON
2. BLAKE
3. BLIGH
4. BORLAS
5. BOROUGH
6. BOSCOWEN
7. BROKE
8. BYRON
9. CAMPERDOWN
10. CAREW
11. CARY
12. CECIL
13. CELY
14. CLIFFORD
15. COLLINGWOOD
16. COOK
17. FRA-DRAKE

PAST

1897

56 39 23 25 28 3 27 17 4 33 18 14 8 16 32 46 54 11 37 54 2 35 6 22 1 58 9 38

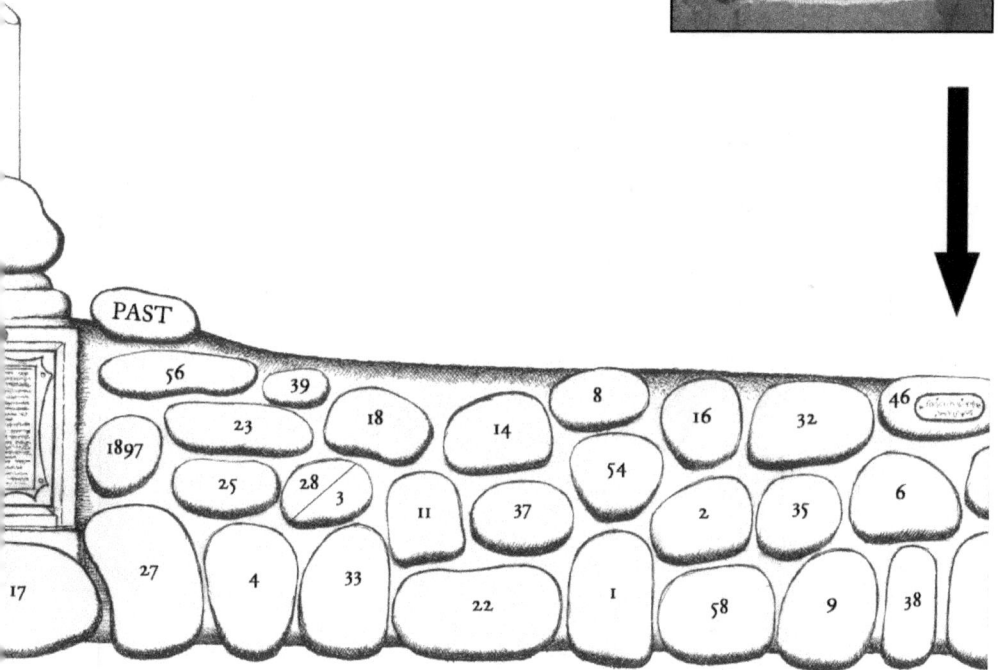

18.	DUDLEY	32.	HAWKE	47.	PENN
19.	DUFF	33.	HAWKINS	48.	POLLWHELY
20.	DUNDONALD	34.	HERBERT	49.	PRESTON
21.	FENNER	35.	HOOD	50.	RALEGH
22.	FENTON	36.	HOSTE	51.	RIOU
23.	FLEMING	37.	HOWARD	52.	RODNEY
24.	FROBISER	38.	HOWE	53.	ROOK
25.	GILBERTIE	39.	KEMY	54.	SAUNDERS
26.	GORGES	40.	KEPPEL	55.	SCOTT
27.	GREYNVILLE	41.	KING	56.	SOUTHWELL
28.	GROSS	42.	LAWRENCE	57.	STAYNER
29.	HARDY	43.	MILLER	58.	ST VINCENT
30.	HARIO	44.	MONCK	59.	VERE
31.	HARVY	45.	NELSON	60.	WHIDDON
		46.	PASCO	61.	WYNTER

CONTENTS

INTRODUCTION

Northam's best kept secret is perhaps the magnificent view of Bideford Bay and Lundy to be had from the small park at Bone Hill behind St Margaret's Church.

At a Parish Council Meeting held on the 26th April 1897 in the National School (now the Community Centre) it was resolved by unanimous vote that the proposal of Captain William Blackeney RN of Hillsborough, Westward Ho! Road be accepted. This called for a permanent memorial to be commissioned, to celebrate the 60 year reign of Her Majesty Queen Victoria. His proposal specified a cairn of 60 stones taken from the Pebble Ridge, surmounted by a splendid flagpole, from which the Union Jack and St George's flag should be flown on the following occasions:-

New Year's Day
The Sovereign's Birthday
The Heir to the Throne's Birthday
Waterloo Day 18th June (1815)
Gravelines Day 13th July (1558)
Trafalgar Day 21st October (1805)
Empire Day 24th May

A great enthusiast of the Royal Navy and its traditions, Captain Blackeney believed it to be most appropriate that each of the 60 stones should be deeply engraved with the name of a Naval hero. And so it was to be.

The finished construction which is enclosed by a neat fence, at first provided an adjacent shelter from the elements which may be seen in old photographs.

I would conjecture that Captain Blackeney produced his list of heroes from memory, and the stonemason believed to be James Edward Gabriel, of 15,

DIAMOND JUBILEE CELEBRATION,

Barnstaple Street, East the Water) interpreted the Captain's copperplate handwriting, so typical of the period, as he thought best, being unfamiliar with the heroes concerned. This would go a long way to account for the eccentric spelling of some of the names.

In the compilation of the following brief biographies I have had to compress many long and action-packed careers into a very few lines, so there will be much I have omitted. There is also one name whose history I cannot locate.

In the tradition of Captain Blackeney and his stonemason, I have trusted to luck in matching the engraved names with the historic record. I hope that I have not exacerbated and compounded existing errors. You shall be my judge.

Jim Jackson
Appledore
20/12

1. ANSON
George Anson – Baron
1697-1762.
Admiral and subsequently First Lord of the Admiralty. During the war of the Austrian Succession he commanded a fleet of six ships in attacks on Spanish South America (1740). He circumnavigated the world, taking four years to do so, losing most of his ships and crew in the process.

He commanded the first British ship to enter China, and returned to Britain with plunder worth £500,000. Upon his return, he told of his adventures in *A Voyage Round the World* published in 1748.

2. BLAKE
Robert Blake
1599 – 1657.
Admiral and Parliamentarian. He was a favourite of Oliver Cromwell. In 1650 he destroyed the Royalist fleet led by Prince Rupert. In the First Dutch War he decisively defeated the Dutch Admiral Tromp at the Battle of Portland. He destroyed a fleet of pirate ships off Tunis in 1655, and sent to the bottom sixteen Spanish ships at Santa-Cruz off Tenerife in 1657. He died on the way home to Plymouth. He is considered by many to be the father of the British Navy.

3. BLIGH
Captain William Bligh – Admiral
1754 – 1817.
He accompanied James Cook on his second voyage around the world. Whatever his skill as a seaman and a navigator, his man-management skills were deplorable. He was involved in three mutinies, the most famous of which landed him in an open boat when the crew of the *Bounty* rebelled. With eighteen loyal crew members he sailed 4,000 miles to Timor, without charts.

4. BORLAS
Sir John Borlase-Warren
1753 – 1822.
Although educated at Cambridge he entered the Navy as an able-bodied seaman in 1771. By 1777 he was a Commodore commanding the squadron blockading Brest, where he is said to have destroyed 220 vessels, and frustrated French plans to invade Ireland. Created an MP and Privy Councillor in 1806. He captured the large French War Ship *Marengo* and was promoted Admiral in 1810.

5. BOROUGH
Stephen Borough
1524 – 1584.
Borough is the first local man commemorated here. He was born in Northam, and in 1553 he took part in the expedition which was dispatched from the Thames under Sir Hugh

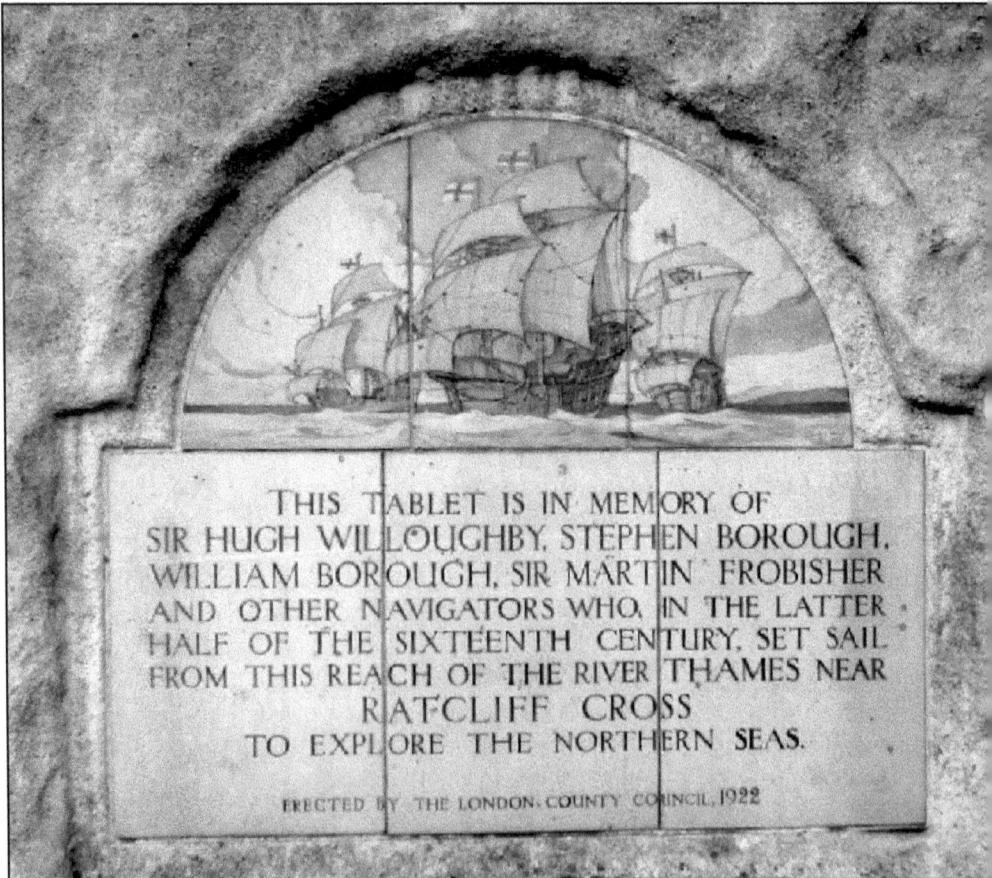

THIS TABLET IS IN MEMORY OF
SIR HUGH WILLOUGHBY, STEPHEN BOROUGH,
WILLIAM BOROUGH, SIR MARTIN FROBISHER
AND OTHER NAVIGATORS WHO, IN THE LATTER
HALF OF THE SIXTEENTH CENTURY, SET SAIL
FROM THIS REACH OF THE RIVER THAMES NEAR
RATCLIFF CROSS
TO EXPLORE THE NORTHERN SEAS.

ERECTED BY THE LONDON COUNTY COUNCIL, 1922

Willoughby to look for a northern passage to Cathay and India. He served as master of the *Edward Bonaventure*, on which Richard Chancellor sailed as pilot in chief. Separated by a storm from the *Bona Esperanza* and the *Bona Confidentia*, the other two ships of the expedition, Borough proceeded on his voyage alone, sailing into the White Sea. In the words of his epitaph, he: "discovered Moscouia by the Northerne [sic] sea passage to St. Nicholas (Archangel)".

6. BOSCOWEN
Edward Boscowen
1711 – 1761.
Admiral and MP for Truro. His engagements include the siege of Louisberg and The Battle of Lagos.

He is also remembered for having signed the Death Warrant of Admiral Bing, after he was court-martialled for having failed to engage the enemy with the necessary vigour. Bing's execution was satirised by Voltaire as something the English do from time to time to encourage the other Admirals. He also served on the Board of Admiralty and as a Privy Councillor.

7. BROKE
Philip Bowes Vere Broke
1776 – 1841.
He joined the Royal Naval Academy at Portsmouth Dockyard in 1788, and began active service as a midshipman in 1792. He served as third lieutenant on the frigate *HMS Southampton* during the Battle of Cape St. Vincent in February 1797. His most notable accomplishment was his victory while commanding *HMS Shannon*, over the *USS Chesapeake* on 1 June 1813, during the War of 1812.

8. BYRON
John Byron
1723 -1786.
Admiral and grandfather of the poet Lord Byron. He had the epithet of 'Foul-Weather Jack'. He joined the navy in 1731, accompanying George Anson on his circumnavigation of the globe as a midshipman. In 1741, Byron's ship, *HMS Wager*, was shipwrecked on the coast of Patagonia, and the survivors decided to divide into two teams, one to make its way by boat to Rio de Janeiro, the other, John Byron's, to sail North. He was appointed Governor of Newfoundland in 1767. By some accounts he was used as the model for Don Juan in the poem by his grandson. He described his adventures in *Mutiny in The Narrative of the Honourable John Byron* (1768).

9. CAMPERDOWN
Admiral Adam Duncan
1731 – 1804.
Camperdown was the scene of a major sea battle (depicted above by Thomas Whitcombe) in 1797. This was between a Royal Naval Fleet under Admiral Adam Duncan and Vice Admiral Jan-de-Winter of the Dutch Navy. The British were victorious, but losses were heavy on both sides. Admiral Duncan was made Baron Duncan of Lundie and Viscount Duncan of Camperdown in November of the same year.

10. CAREW
George Carew
1555 – 1629.
A distinguished soldier and administrator. From an old Devonshire family, he was appointed Lieutenant General of Ordinance in 1592, and accompanied Robert Devereux on his Naval raid on Cadiz in 1596, and to the Azores in 1597.

He fought unsuccessfully to prevent the execution of his close friend Sir Walter Raleigh. He was made Earl of Totnes in 1626.

11. CARY
Sir George Carey – 2nd Baron Hudson
1547 – 1603.
An unusual choice of Naval hero. During the Armada emergency he commanded Carisbrooke Castle on the Isle of Wight, and was never in danger. He died in 1603 of venereal disease and mercury poisoning; the latter being the standard medication for the complaint at that time.

12. CECIL
Sir William Cecil – Lord Burley
1520 – 1598.
Cecil was an English statesman, the chief advisor of Queen Elizabeth I for most of her reign, twice Secretary of State (1550–1553 and 1558–1572) and Lord High Treasurer from 1572. He was the founder of the Cecil dynasty which has produced many politicians including two prime ministers. His network of spies on the Continent kept the Admiralty fully appraised of Spanish preparations for the proposed invasion of England.

13. CELY
Captain Thomas Cely
Dates uncertain
A merchant adventurer and captain of the 100 ton *Minion,* he accompanied Drake and 22 other ships on his raiding expedition to the West Indies in 1585/6. Captured and brought before the Inquisition, he was sentenced to servitude aboard a Spanish Galley. Upon his escape or release he returned to Britain with vital intelligence concerning Spanish plans for invasion. He fought beside Drake against the Spanish Armada (pictured here by Cornelis Claesz van Wieringen) and later had the unalloyed satisfaction of de-bagging eight Spanish Officers held captive in Bridewell Prison.

14. CLIFFORD
George Clifford – 3rd Earl of Cumberland
1558 – 1605.

Whilst having little success commanding the 47 Gun *Elizabeth Adventura* during the Anglo Spanish War he had better fortune in the Caribbean aboard his own ship, *Scourge of Malice*. He is famous for his short lived 1598 capture of Fort San Felipe del Morro, the citadel protecting San Juan, Puerto Rico. He arrived in Puerto Rico on June 15, 1598, but by November of that year, Clifford and his men had fled the island due to harsh civilian resistance.

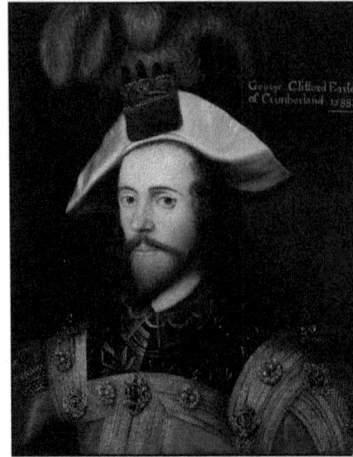

He later made quite a fortune, but lost it gambling on horses and jousting. He helped to set up the East India Company.

15. COLLINGWOOD
Cuthbert Collingwood 1st Baron
1750 – 1810.

At the age of twelve, he went to sea on the frigate *HMS Shannon*. After several years of service and a short period attached to *HMS Lenox*, he sailed to Boston in 1774 on *HMS Preston*. He fought at the battle of Bunker Hill in June 1775, and was commissioned as a Lieutenant. He saw action during the American Revolutionary War and the Napoleonic Wars. He fought with distinction at the Battle of the 'Glorious First of June' 1794 and Cape St Vincent 1797. After Nelson's death at Trafalgar he succeeded to his Command. Upon his own death in 1810 he was buried beside Nelson in St Paul's Cathedral.

16. COOK
Captain James Cook
1728 – 1779.

Navigator and Cartographer. An experienced seaman, he joined the Royal Navy in 1755 and saw active service in the Seven Years' War, during which time he surveyed the Saint Lawrence River. From his observation of the lunar eclipse came his Commission to Tahiti to observe the transit of Venus. He went on to discover Australia in 1768, and then New Zealand. In proposing a diet high in vitamin C he saved many lives from scurvy. His second voyage was in 1772-5 aboard *The Adventure* during

which he circumnavigated the Antarctic, discovering Easter Island, New Caledonia, the South Sandwich Islands and South Georgia. On his third voyage, on the Big Island of Hawaii he was murdered by savages with whom relations had previously been cordial.

17. FRA DRAKE
Sir Francis Drake
1540 -1596.
Perhaps the most famous English Admiral of his period. He circumnavigated the world in his ship *The Pelican* (re-named *The Golden Hind*). He played a major role in the defeat of the Spanish Armada, and was a thorn in the side of the Spanish for many years. His last voyage was against Spanish possessions in the West Indies, where he died. He was buried at sea in a lead lined coffin off Portobello, Panama.

18. DUDLEY
Sir Robert Dudley
1574 – 1649.
A polymath - sailor, engineer, writer and shipbuilder, he spent much of his life trying to prove his right to the titles of Duke of Northumberland and Earl of Warwick. He was famous for his great work 'Secrets of the Sea' which contained the sum of contemporary knowledge of navigation, and was also author of many learned works on shipbuilding and navigation. He was knighted for his part in the War against Spain. In 1594, Dudley assembled a fleet of ships, intending to use them to harass the Spaniards in the Atlantic. The Queen did not approve of his plans because of his inexperience and the value of the ships. She commissioned him as a general, but instead insisted that he sail to Guiana.

19. DUFF
George Duff
1764 -1805.
A professional seaman from a young age, he took part in the Seige of Gibraltar, and went on to see a great deal of action in his country's service. However he did not receive the honours and recognition which some of his peers attracted. Following the Peace of Amiens he was given command of *HMS Mars*. Nelson gave him charge of the inshore Squadron at Trafalgar, where he fell, decapitated by French roundshot from shore-based artillery.

20. DUNDONALD
Thomas Cochrane – 10th Earl Dundonald
1775 – 1860.

A captain during the Napoleonic Wars who earned for himself the nickname 'Le Loup Des Mers' [The Sea Wolf]. He was dismissed by the Navy following a conviction for fraud and wandered the world in search of gainful employment.

Returning home he received a pardon and was re-instated as Rear Admiral of the Blue, later rising to the Admiral of the Red (Admiral of the Fleet). He is believed to have been the inspiration for C.S. Forester's 'Horatio Hornblower'.

21. FENNER

There were two Fenners who served in the English fleet which set out to attack Spain after the defeat of the Armada. Edward Fenner who commanded the *Swiftsure* (see below) and Thomas Fenner who commanded the *Dreadnought*.

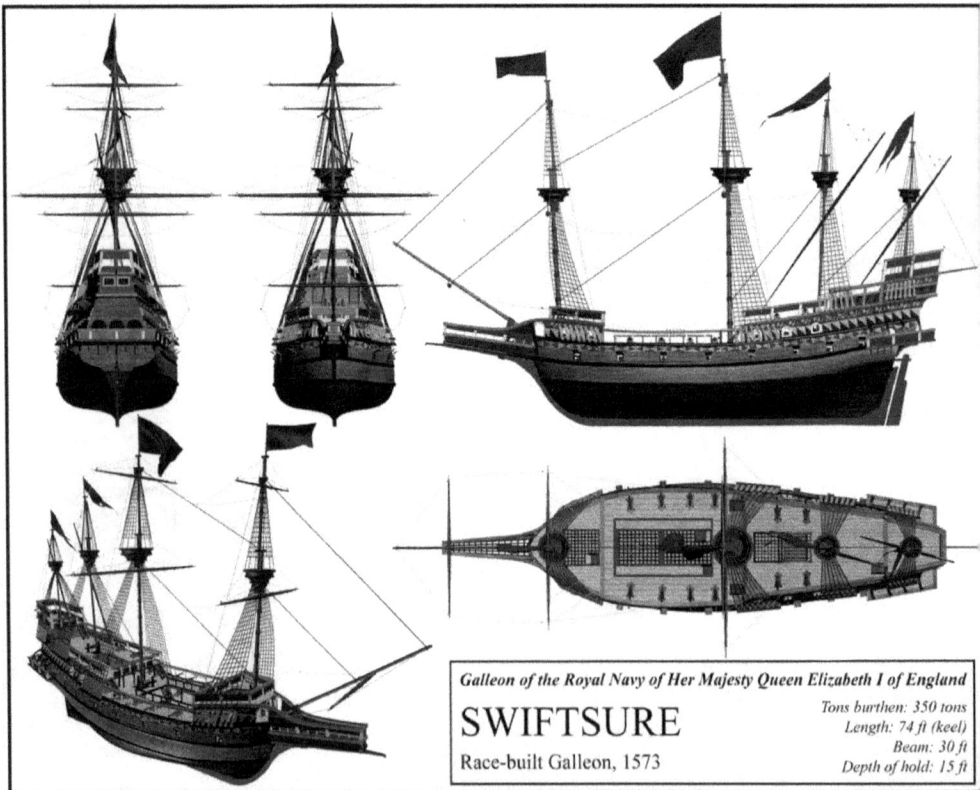

Galleon of the Royal Navy of Her Majesty Queen Elizabeth I of England

SWIFTSURE
Race-built Galleon, 1573

Tons burthen: 350 tons
Length: 74 ft (keel)
Beam: 30 ft
Depth of hold: 15 ft

22. FENTON
Edward Fenton
c1555 – 1603.
He sailed with Frobisher's second expedition to find the North West Passage. The map shown here was the first map to show the North Pole and, although not completed until three years after Fenton's death, was partly based on cartographical data brought back from the voyage. In 1558 Fenton was given command of *HMS Mary Rose* (not to be confused with her illustrious predecessor) one of the fleet which set sail to oppose the Spanish Armada.

23. FLEMING
Richard Howell Fleming
1778 – 1856.
He entered the Navy in 1793 and saw action in the reduction of The French West Indies possessions. He served in many other expeditions and was wounded on more than one occasion. He was Commander [2ic] on *HMS Ocean* (pictured right), a Guard Ship based in Sheerness between 1843 and 1846. If anyone can help the publishers find a photograph of him, please get in touch.

24. FROBISER
Sir Martin Frobisher
1535 – 1594.
An early explorer of the North East coast of Canada, he investigated the possibility of finding a North West sea route to the Pacific and the East. Frobisher Bay in Canada was named after him. He brought back samples of what he believed to be gold ore, but it turned out to be useless iron pyrite (iron sulphide), also known as 'Fool's Gold'.

In 1585 he was Vice Admiral to Drake's expedition to the West Indies, and later played a prominent part in the defeat of the Spanish Armada, for which he was knighted.

In 1594 he was involved in the relief of Brest, during which he was shot; a wound which eventually led to his death several days later.

25. GILBERTE
Sir Humphrey Gilbert
1539 – 1583.
Soldier and navigator.

The step-brother of Sir Walter Raleigh, he proposed many grand plans for the colonisation of North America. In June 1583 he sailed for Newfoundland, which he claimed for Britain on the 3rd August. A month later he sailed for home. He was last sighted on the frigate *Squirrel,* sitting in the stern reading a book. He was heard to cry out repeatedly, *"We are as near to Heaven by sea as by land!"* as he lifted his palm to the skies to illustrate his point, and was never seen again.

26. GORGES
Arthur Gorges
1569 – 1625.
A cousin of Sir Walter Raleigh. In 1597 he commanded the *War-spite* in which Walter Raleigh sailed as Vice Admiral under the Earl of Essex. He was a relative of Fernando Gorges, who founded the State of Maine but never set foot there. He was a well known poet and author, and much to our surprise we have not been able to find a picture of him. Perhaps *you* can help?

27. GREYNVILLE *
Sir Richard Grenville
1542 – 1591.
Given to fight against impossible odds Grenville first achieved fame in fighting the Spanish Fleet off the Azores. In 1585 he commanded an expedition carrying 100 colonists to Roanoke, North Carolina. In 1591 he led a squadron of 15 ships to capture the Spanish treasure fleet. When 53 Spanish vessels approached he found himself cut off, and fought for 15 hours until his ship was captured along with its 150 man crew. It took 15 galleons and 5000 men to do it. A few days later Sir Richard died of his wounds.

* Note – Following a period of extensive and scholarly research Appledore author and historian David Carter has recently positively identified Sir Richard Grenville's home in Bideford at 1 – 5 Bridge Street. The house has now been earmarked as a Museum and Heritage Centre.

28. GROSS
Sir Robert Cross
1552 – 1611

A professional seaman who commanded the 600 ton *Hope* (similar to the one pictured here) against the Spanish Armada. He was knighted by Robert Devereux Second Earl of Essex in 1596 on behalf of Queen Elizabeth I for the part he played in the capture of Cadiz. From 1598 he commanded the *Vanguard*.

29. HARDY
Sir Thomas Masterman Hardy – Baronet
1769 – 1839.

Friends with Nelson since 1795 he subsequently commanded two of his flagships during the French Revolutionary and the Napoleonic Wars. After the Battle of the Nile in 1798 he was appointed to command Nelson's flagship *HMS Vanguard*. He was also Captain of the *HMS Victory*, and was at Nelson's side as he lay mortally wounded at Trafalgar. Nelson's last words were "Kiss me Hardy" (possibly "Kismet Hardy"). Made a Baronet in 1806, he became First Sea Lord in 1830 and was appointed Vice Admiral. From 1834 until his death, he was the governor of the Naval Hospital, Greenwich.

30. HARIO
Thomas Harlot
1560 – 1621.

In an age when sailors were only just learning to navigate accurately over long distances, he was retained as a scientific advisor by Sir Walter Raleigh to his 1585/6 expedition to Roanoke, North Carolina. He advised on the design of his ships and the best way to store ammunition. By some accounts it was he who brought the potato to Britain. He spent a long time and demonstrated great patience in learning to communicate with the Native-American Manteo, and transcribed the Algonquail language into English. His books on mathematics and navigation continued to be published for many years after his death.

31. HARVY
Sir John Harvey
1740 – 1794.

Sir John had a long and varied career in numerous ships during which time he somehow managed to raise a large family (which included many future Admirals.) He saw active service in the American War of Independence and in the French Revolutionary Wars.

He played a noble part in The Battle of 1st June, sustaining three wounds from musket ball, roundshot and splinter. He survived the Battle but his injuries were to prove fatal. His memorial can be seen in Westminster Abbey.

32. HAWKE
Edward Hawke – Baron
1705 – 1781.

In October 1747 he captured six French warships off the coast of Brittany.

His victory at Quiberon Bay in 1759 put an end to French plans to invade Britain. He was promoted to Rear Admiral for his services in the War of the Austrian Succession.

He served as lst Sealord of the Admiralty from 1766 – 1771, and was elevated to the Peerage as a Baron in 1776.

33. HAWKINS
Sir John Hawkins
1532 – 1598.

Largely due to his influence the Elizabethan Navy was reconfigured with a view to seriously disrupting Spain's trade with the New World, a process in which his kinsman Drake played a prominent part. He lost all but two of his six ships when ambushed by superior Spanish forces off the coast of Veracruz. However both he and Drake escaped to fight another day. He had his revenge in exposing Spain's part in the Ridolfi plot to depose Queen Elizabeth I and install Mary Stuart on the English Throne. He was third in command of the ships which defeated the Spanish Armada. In company with Drake he planned a raid on Puerto Rico but died shortly before the attack was due to take place.

34. HERBERT
Sir Arthur Herbert
1648 – 1716 1st Earl of Torrington.
During the reign of William and Mary he served as Lord High Admiral and then First Lord of the Admiralty. He commanded the English and Dutch fleets at the Battle of Beachy Head in 1690 where he was seriously defeated by the French.

Herbert was imprisoned and court-martialled, but acquitted. An enigmatic character who it is alleged was partial to strong drink and the company of loose women even when at sea, he was a strange choice of hero to be lauded by a Victorian Captain, but - again - perhaps not.

35. HOOD
Samuel Hood – 1st Viscount
1724 – 1816.
Admiral. A genuine fighting sailor who rose to eminence during the American Revolutionary War. He defeated the French off the coast of Dominica in 1782. During the French Revolutionary Wars he captured Toulon in 1793 and destroyed the defences of Corsica in 1794.

36. HOSTE
Captain Sir William Hoste
1780-1828.
One of the best known of Nelson's protégés whose career is an essay in itself of loyal service, adventure and subsequent promotion. He entered the Navy at the tender age of five, as a captain's servant aboard *HMS Europa*. He went on to see service on many ships, including *HMS Agamemnon*, *HMS Captain* at the Battle of Cape St Vincent and *HMS Thesius* at the Battle of the Nile.

Hoste was given the command of *HMS Bacchante*, and continued to demonstrate the same kind of initiative and aggression as before.

He also took an active part in the capture of Rome in 1799. At about this time he contracted tuberculosis which coupled with malaria led to his death. He was made a Baronet in 1815.

37. HOWARD
Charles Howard of Effingham – Second Baron
1536 – 1624.

As Lord High Admiral he commanded the British Fleet to victory over the Spanish Armada (with a little help from the weather), Howard was created Earl of Nottingham in 1596 and was appointed Lord Lieutenant General of England. In the same year, when another Spanish invasion was feared, Howard was again appointed to defend England. Howard and the Earl of Essex jointly led an attack against the Spanish base at Cadiz on June 20. However, in 1601, the Earl of Essex rebelled, and Howard took command of the soldiers massed to defend London, and defeated his old comrade in the field.

Howard served as a commissioner at Essex's trial and examined him at least once. Howard served on the commission of union between England and Scotland. He also served on the Gunpowder Plot trial in 1605.

38. HOWE
Richard Howe – Earl
1726 – 1799.

An Admiral in the Seven Years' War he served with great distinction off the north French coast. Commander of the British Fleet during the American Revolutionary War he is best remembered for his victory over the French at the Battle of 'The Glorious 1st of June' 1794. His brother also achieved fame during the American Revolutionary War but lost it after his failure at Valley Forge in 1778.

39. KEMY
Lawrence Kemys
c 1580 – 1618.

Kemys sailed as Raleigh's right hand man to Guiana in search of the gold which might possibly reinstate him at court upon his return, as Raleigh was under a suspended death sentence at that time. Acting on his own initiative, and against all orders, Kemys attacked the Spanish settlement at Santo Tome on the river Orinoco. During this engagement Raleigh's son, Watt was killed. Raleigh never forgave Kemys on either account. Kemys, knowing that his precipitate action in defiance of direct orders from the Crown would cost Raleigh his head, took his own life with a pistol and a knife. Hardly an heroic exemplar to grace a monument to a queen.

40. KEPPEL
Augustus Kepple
1725 -1786.

Although a sailor since the age of ten, and one who served in both the American Revolutionary War and the Seven Years' War in Europe, he was more politician than sailor. A leading Whig member of the House of Commons, he frequently came into conflict with the 4th Earl of Sandwich. Discharged from his command in 1779, he eventually became 1st Sealord in 1782 following America's victory and the fall of Lord North's administration.

41. KING
Richard King
1774 – 1834.

As Captain of *HMS Sirus* he captured four enemy privateers. He sat on the Navy Board which sentenced Richard Parker to death for his part in the Nore Mutiny.

In 1798 he captured 2 Dutch ships and was rewarded with command of *HMS Archille*. He fought at Trafalgar oddly fighting the French *Archilles* which was forced to surrender. Made Rear Admiral and 2nd in Command to Pellew, he was also appointed KCB. After a long fighting career he eventually fell to cholera in Sheerness.

42. LAWRENCE
No trace

43. MILLER
Ralph Willett Miller
1762 – 1799.

During the American Revolutionary War, his family lost everything as they had remained loyal to Britain. He entered the Navy in 1778. Promoted by Rodney, he served under Hood. After the siege of Toulon he was moved to *HMS Victory,* after which he held a number of commands including command of *HMS Captain*, which was Nelson's flagship (seen here capturing the Spanish ships *San Nicolas* and *San Josef* at the Battle of Cape St Vincent, 14 February 1797).

He fought aboard *HMS Vanguard* at the Battle of the Nile where he was wounded. With his wounds still not totally healed, he was subsequently sent to Gibraltar under the avuncular eye of Captain James de Saumarez, who had command of French prizes. Returning to the eastern Mediterranean under Sir Sidney Smith, he died in an unfortunate accident whilst about to set sail in pursuit of a number of French supply ships, then leaving Alexandria.

44. MONCK

George Monck – 1st Duke of Albermarle
1608 – 1670.
A General during the Civil War, he was initially a Royalist, but was captured and changed sides. In the first Dutch War he became a successful General at Sea (a title which preceded Admiral).

He supported the overthrow of Richard Cromwell, opposed the Military Government which followed and was influential in the restoration of Charles II.

45. NELSON

Horatio Nelson – Admiral
1758 – 1805.
At the commencement of the French Revolutionary War he was given command of the *Agamemnon* at Calvi. In 1794 he lost the sight in his right eye. He went on to play an important part in the victory of Cape St Vincent, for which he was knighted.

Having subsequently lost his right arm, he went on to victory at the Battle of the Nile.

In 1801 he was given command of the Baltic Fleet and secured a notable victory at Copenhagen.

In 1803 he returned to the Mediterranean, blockaded Toulon for 18 months, but the French escaped.

He followed and joined them in battle at Trafalgar in 1805 aboard *HMS Victory* where he fell and subsequently died of his wounds (pictured above by Benjamin West). He is buried in St Paul's Cathedral.

46. PASCO

John Pasco

1774 – 1853.

He entered the Navy as a Captain's Servant and served under Prince William Henry (later William IV). After seeing action in many ships he joined *HMS Victory* in 1803. It was he who as Signals Officer caused the famous command to be hoisted 'England Expects This Day That Every Man Will Do His Duty'.

In 1846 he was given command of *HMS Victory* at Portsmouth and appointed Rear Admiral the following year.

47. PENN
Admiral Sir William Penn
1621-1670.

He first saw service under Cromwell in the Mediterranean and South Atlantic, in pursuit of Royalists. In the first Anglo-Dutch war he commanded a squadron at the Battle of Kentish Knock. Later he launched a failed attack on Hispaniola, but seized Jamaica instead. On his return to Britain he was imprisoned in the tower but later released to become an MP after the Restoration.

He worked with Samuel Pepys on the Naval Board who mentions him frequently in his diary. Not a man of high political ideals perhaps, but a determined survivor in turbulent times. Nevertheless he was a man who exercised a great and enduring influence over the creed and tactics of the Royal Navy (note that his son - a pacifist and Quaker - founded the Commonwealth of Pennsylvania).

48. POLLWHELY
Captain William Polwhely.
There is little record of the heroic deeds of this officer who served in the Navy that defeated the Spanish Armada, except that he married Mary Filton, a maid of honour to Queen Elizabeth I in 1607. A deed which perhaps took more courage than we may imagine.

49. PRESTON
Sir Amyas Preston
c 1550 – 1617.
He first saw service as a lieutenant aboard the *Ark Royal* in action against the Spanish Armada. He subsequently plundered the Spanish Main in company with George Summers. He did considerable damage to Spanish possessions, but without much personal profit.

In 1596 as Captain of the *Ark Royal* (right) he was knighted for his services at Cadiz. He was keeper of the Ordnance at the Tower of London from 1603 until his death.

50. RALEGH
Sir Walter Raleigh
1554 – 1618.

Explorer and adventurer. His attempt to found a colony in America was unsuccessful, but he brought back the potato and tobacco. In 1595/6 he led an expedition to South America, and in 1596 took part in the sack of Cadiz. In 1603 he stood trial for treason. He was released from the tower in 1616 to search for gold up the Orinoco, but his expedition was a failure, and upon his return to England his death sentence was invoked and he was executed.

51. RIOU
Edward Riou
1762 – 1801.

He served as a midshipman on Captain James Cook's third and final voyage of discovery. His first command was the former frigate *Guardian,* by then a convict ship which hit an iceberg and was abandoned by most of its crew. With his vessel barely afloat, he navigated it to safety, saving many lives. His bravery and tenacity earned him promotion and command. He served under Hyde Parker and commanded Nelson's frigate squadron during the Battle of Copenhagen, where he was cut down by fire from shore based artillery. His monument may be seen in St Paul's Cathedral.

52. RODNEY
George Brydges Rodney – 1st Baron – Admiral
1718 -1792.

He wrecked a French invasion fleet during the 7 Years' War, and won victories against countries supporting the American cause during the American Revolution. His victory over the French off the coast of Dominica in 1782 greatly strengthened Britain's negotiating hand at the peace negotiations at Versailles in 1783. To some Rodney was a controversial figure, accused of an obsession with prize money. This was brought to a head in the wake of his taking of the Caribbean island of Sint Eustatius for which he was heavily criticised in Britain. On his return to Britain, Rodney was made a peer. He lived in retirement until his death in 1792. The use of Rodney as a first name originates with the admiral. It became a popular name for boys at the end of the eighteenth century.

53. ROOK
Sir George Rooke
1650 -1709.

At the Battle of Vigo Bay during the War of the Spanish Succession in 1702 he destroyed the Spanish Treasure fleet. In May 1692 he served under Russell at the Battle of Barfleur, and he greatly distinguished himself in a night attack on the French fleet at La Hogue, when he succeeded in burning twelve of their ships. He was knighted shortly afterwards. He commanded the allied Naval Fleet at the capture of Gibraltar, becoming the military governor for a few weeks. A statue in his honour was raised in Gibraltar in 2004 during the 300th anniversary celebrations.

54. SAUNDERS
Sir Charles Saunders
1715 – 1775.

He commanded the fleet which took James Wolf to Quebec.

In 1760 he resumed his role as Commander in Chief of the Mediterranean Fleet and blockaded Cadiz. Cape Saunders in New Zealand was named in his honour by James Cook who served under him in Canada. He was a Royal Navy officer in the Royal Navy during the Seven Years' War and later served as First Lord of the Admiralty. He was appointed to the Privy Council in 1766.

55. SCOTT
(a late addition to the memorial)
Robert Falcon Scott
1858 – 1912.

He joined the Royal Navy in 1881 and was promoted to Captain in 1904. In 1910 he embarked on his Second Antarctic Expedition, but was beaten to the South Pole by Roald Amundsen. The return journey was terrible, and even the courageous self-sacrifice of Captain L.E.G. Oates did not ameliorate the hopeless situation. Shortly after his last diary entry on the 29th March 1912, Scott died of exhaustion, cold and hunger and no doubt of disappointment also.

56. SOUTHWELL

Sir Robert Southwell
1563 – 1598.

Such was his reputation as a seaman, that he was given command of the *Elizabeth Jonas* (right) which at 900 tons, 56 guns and a crew of 500 was one of the largest warships in Elizabeth's Navy. He participated in the raid upon Cadiz, and was knighted for his services on the 18th June 1585 and was promoted to Vice Admiral the same year.

In company with a powerful squadron, he pursued the rags of the Armada out into the North Sea. But of his large crew, 300 died of an unspecified sickness. This caused him to break off the chase. He fumigated his ship by burning broom clippings, and the disease abated.

57. STAYNER

Sir Richard Stayner
1624 – 1662.

He saw distinguished action in the First Dutch War and was promoted to Rear Admiral of the Fleet in 1660. On 22 June 1649 he was appointed commander of the *Elizabeth*. A prize, 'now a State's ship,' though a very small one, her principal armament being two sakers, that is, six-pounders. In August he captured the *Robert*, a small frigate, apparently one of Prince Rupert's vessels, for which and other good services he was awarded a gold medal (*ib.* 13 April 1650). Knighted by both Cromwell and Charles II, and his picture hangs in the National Portrait Gallery.

58. ST VINCENT

Sir John Jervis. 1st Earl St Vincent.
1735 - 1823.

An able administrator who served with Cook and Wolf at the Seige of Quebec. Upon being given command of the Channel Fleet, he sought to impose his own very strict forms of discipline, and turned to Thomas Troubridge and James de Saumarez, two trusted Captains from the Mediterranean Fleet, to enforce them. Described as an "organiser of victories, and the creator of highly efficient fleets", he was assuredly a good friend to efficient officers, but a deadly enemy to those less than assiduous in the performance of their duties.

59. VERE
Sir Francis Vere
1560 -1609.

The young Francis Vere first went on active service under Leicester in 1585, and was soon in the thick of the war raging in the Low Countries. At the siege of Sluys he greatly distinguished himself under Sir Roger Williams and Sir Thomas Baskerville. Renowned as one of the best soldiers of his generation, he served in the Cadiz expedition of 1596. He negotiated the Anglo-Dutch Alliance and obtained the Governorship of Brill. He attained the rank of General and became MP for Leominster in 1593.

Sr Francis Veer Colonel et Gouverneur d'Oostende.

60. WHIDDON
Jacob Whiddon
c 1560 – 1595.

He commanded Raleigh's ship *Roebuck* against the Spanish Armada, where it was employed in scouting duties, and helped in the capture of the galleon *Rosary*. He took from her ten cannon, and several tons of gunpowder, which although of inferior quality was much needed by the English fleet. He took possession of, and brought into Torbay, the flagship of Don Pedro de Valdes; (whose surrender is pictured below). He brought supplies of ammunition to the fleet, and was constantly employed in scouting duty.

61. WYNTER
William Wynter
1519 -1589.

Keeper of the King's Naval Storehouse at Deptford. Surveyor of the Navy. Participated in the Battle of Gravelines. Vice Admiral of England He was granted the Mayor of Lydney in recognition of his many services to the realm. The *Mynyon* (right) was William Wynter's command in 1552, and used in the evacuation of French troops from the Siege of Leith in 1560

CAPTAIN WILLIAM BLACKENEY
1835 -1912

'*AUXILIUM MEUM AB ALTO*'

He served aboard *HMS Acteon* during its survey tour of the Far East.

His book *On the Coasts of Cathay and Cipango* published by Elliott Stock (1902) is still available as an e-book.

Upon retirement he made his home at Hillsborough, Westward Ho! Road. A plaque to his memory may be seen on the east wall of St Georges Chapel in St Margaret's Church, but perhaps a more apposite memorial may be found in the depiction of the flagpole he inspired upon Northam's Mayorial Chain.

POSTSCRIPT

I n an age where Britain's pride in its heritage and institutions are increasingly treated with cynical indifference, disdain, or hostility, it is heartening to learn that Northam Town Council is to reintroduce the custom of flag raising at Bone Hill in accordance with the schedule of dates proposed by Captain Blackeney on the occasion of Queen Victoria's Diamond Jubilee.

In this, the Jubilee Year of our own Queen Elizabeth II, it might be considered fitting to celebrate her Reign and the victories of the 20th Century in the same fashion. The Battle of Passchendaele, The Battle of Britain, The Normandy Campaign, and the Liberation of The Falklands being obvious contenders of mark. Pivotal as these battles were, to remember them and those who served in isolation, would - I feel - in some way marginalise those who saw action in other conflicts, which in human terms were no less costly.

With this in mind I would suggest that the flag be raised on 11th November - Armistice Day each year; this being a most suitable remembrance of our way of life and of all those who gave so much to preserve it.

J.W.J.

Now the labourer's task is o'er;
Now the battle day is past;
Now upon the farther shore
Lands the voyager at last.

From a hymn by
John Ellerton (1875)

www.ingramcontent.com/pod-product-compliance
Lightning Source LLC
Chambersburg PA
CBHW051050030426
42339CB00006B/287